I0560355

A PRACTICAL GUIDE TO LEADING WITH
SUPPORT, STRIVE, STANDARDS, AND SUCCESS

THE 4S

FRAMEWORK
BY
STACIE SELISE™

LEADERSHIP
WORKBOOK

STACIE SELISE SHANNON

The 4S Framework by Stacie Selise Leadership Workbook
A Companion to the Masterclass in Leadership Playbook
by Stacie Selise
Lead with Power. Live with Purpose.

Copyright © 2025 Stacie Selise LLC. All rights reserved.

No part of this publication may be copied, reproduced, stored in a retrieval system, or transmitted in any form or by any means, electronic, mechanical, photocopying, recording, scanning, or otherwise, without prior written permission from the author, except in brief excerpts for reviews or educational use.

The 4S Framework by Stacie Selise™ is a claimed trademark of Stacie Selise. A federal trademark application is currently pending. Unauthorized use of this name or any derivative material based on this framework is strictly prohibited.

This book is a work of authorship based on personal leadership experiences. Any similarities to other frameworks are purely coincidental.

For permissions, licensing, or publishing inquiries, visit www.stacieselise.com.

Table of Contents

Introduction

Welcome to The 4S Framework by Stacie Selise Leadership Workbook

You're here because you don't just want to *lead*, you want to leave a mark.

This workbook is designed to help you go deeper with the 4S Framework: Support, Strive, Standards, and Success; so you can turn principles into practice, and insight into leadership impact.

Everything inside this guide was created from real experiences. Lived lessons. Unfiltered leadership.

Use it to reflect, plan, and recommit to the version of yourself you've been called to lead with.

You don't need permission. You just need the right framework.

Let's get to work.

With purpose,

Stacie Selise

SECTION 1:

Grounding Your Leadership Identity

"Before you can lead others, you have to know who you are when no one's watching."

—Stacie Selise

Worksheet 1:
Your Leadership Vision

✦ Describe the kind of leader you are today. Be honest. Where are you thriving? Where are you growing?

_____

_____

_____

_____

✦ Now complete the sentence below:
When people experience my leadership, I want them to feel

_____

_____

_____

_____

✦ Now describe the leader you are becoming. How does that version of you lead? How do they talk? How do they show up? What do they let go of? What do they protect?

_____

_____

_____

_____

Worksheet 2:
Values Alignment Activity

Circle your top 5 values from this list:

Integrity	Discipline
Respect	Balance
Freedom	Justice
Growth	Love
Collaboration	Ambition
Excellence	Trust
Faith	Service
Innovation	Peace
Wealth	Energy
Power	

✦ Then narrow your list down to your top 3 leader-ship values:

_____

_____

_____

_____

✦ How do you live each one out in your leadership today? Write a quick note beside each about how it shows up, or where it needs more attention.

_____

_____

_____

_____

Worksheet 3: Strengths & Blind Spots

✦ List 3 leadership strengths you've been praised for.

_____

_____

_____

_____

✦ Now list 1 or 2 areas that challenge you, or that you know need growth.

_____

_____

_____

_____

✦ What are you doing to protect your blind spots?
  Who helps you stay accountable?

_____

_____

_____

_____

Worksheet 4:
Define Your Leadership Voice

Complete these statements:

- My leadership voice is

_____

_____

_____

(inspirational, direct, calm, bold, nurturing, etc.)

- I lead best when I'm

_____

_____

_____

- I lose my voice when

_____

_____

_____

- When I'm grounded in my power, I

_____

_____

_____

- The one word that defines my presence is

_____

_____

_____

SECTION 2:

Activating Support

Lead People, Not Just Performance.

Worksheet 1:
Your Support Style Audit

Respond honestly to the following questions. This is your personal leadership checkpoint.

✦ Do your team members feel comfortable coming to you with challenges?

_____

_____

_____

✦ When was the last time you asked someone, "What do you need from me right now?"

_____

_____

_____

✦ Have you created psychological safety where people can speak without fear?

_____

_____

_____

✦ Do you check in on people as humans, or only when something is wrong?

_____

_____

_____

✦ Do you *model* support, or do you just expect it from others?

_____

_____

_____

Reflection:

Where are you leading with strong support?

_____

_____

_____

Where do you need to be more intentional?

_____

_____

_____

Worksheet 2: Building Psychological Safety

Scenario Exercise:

Read each situation and jot down how you would respond as a supportive leader.

✦ A high performer is suddenly disengaged and quiet during meetings.
  What would you say? What would you do?

_____

_____

_____

✦ A team member made a visible mistake during a major presentation.
  How do you address it while protecting their confidence?

_____

_____

_____

✦ You notice two employees aren't collaborating well. How do you create space for honest feedback without causing shame or division?

_____

_____

_____

Worksheet 3:
Team Mapping Exercise

Think about the key people you lead or work closely with. Fill in their names and note the kind of support they may need right now (emotional, developmental, strategic, practical, etc.)

Name	Role or Relationship	Type of Support They May Need	What I Can Do This Week
Example: *Jordan*	*Project Manager*	*Developmental (public speaking)*	*Invite them to present in next huddle*

Worksheet 4:
Support in Action Plan

This week I will:

☐ Offer support to someone in need
    Model vulnerability in my own leadership

☐ Listen without trying to fix

☐ Check in without checking up

☐ Make space for someone to grow

My "Support in Action" Focus This Week:

What is *one* intentional thing you will do this week to lead with more support?

_____

_____

_____

_____

SECTION 3:

Embracing the Strive Mindset

Lead with Excellence. Move with Heart.

Worksheet 1:
Heart Work vs. Hard Work

Striving isn't just about doing more. It's about doing what matters, with heart.

✦ In your own words, what does striving mean to you?

_____

_____

_____

_____

✦ List 3 things you've done recently that were heart-led, not just hard.

_____

_____

_____

_____

✦ What's one area where you've been working
hard, but not with heart?

_____

_____

_____

_____

✦ What needs to shift?

_____

_____

_____

_____

Worksheet 2:
Strive Tracker – Weekly Excellence Habits

Check off what you've practiced in the last 7 days. Circle any areas that need more intention next week.

- ☐ Spoke up when it mattered

- ☐ Delivered on a promise I made to myself

- ☐ Asked for feedback

- ☐ Pushed through doubt

- ☐ Protected my peace

- ☐ Encouraged someone else

- ☐ Revisited a personal or professional goal

- ☐ Took time to reflect

- ☐ Took care of my body

- ☐ Took care of my energy

My Weekly Strive Summary:

What did striving look like for you this week?

_____

_____

_____

_____

Worksheet 3:
Be Where Your Feet Are

Calendar Alignment Exercise

If your calendar reflects what you *value* most, does it align with your priorities?

Area of Life	Hours Last Week	Does This Reflect What Matters to Me?	Notes / Adjustments Needed
Work / Business			
Health / Wellness			
Family / Relationships			
Self-Care / Rest			
Creative Time / Learning			

Where do you need to show up more intentionally this week?

_____

_____

_____

_____

Worksheet 4:
Boundaries + Breakthroughs

Sometimes striving requires saying no so we can protect our yes.

✦ List 3 boundaries you are committed
   to upholding

_____

_____

_____

✦ List 3 things you are no longer carrying for others,
   your past self, or your old identity

_____

_____

_____

✦ List one breakthrough you're making room for

_____

_____

_____

_____

SECTION 4:
Holding the Standard

Raise It. Communicate It. Protect It.

Worksheet 1: Culture Check. Do Your Standards Show Up?

Answer each question honestly. These will guide your leadership calibration.

✦ Do people know what your standards are without being told?

_____

_____

_____

_____

✦ When standards are broken, do you address it immediately or let it build up?

_____

_____

_____

_____

✦ Are you more consistent in enforcing standards with top performers or struggling ones?

_____

_____

_____

_____

✦ Do your actions reflect the same level of expectation you set for others?

_____

_____

_____

_____

✦ What's one area where your team knows the
   standard clearly?

_____

_____

_____

_____

✦ Where is clarity still missing?

_____

_____

_____

_____

Worksheet 2: Define Your Non-Negotiables

As a leader, there are values and behaviors you cannot afford to compromise.

✦ List 3 leadership non-negotiables you uphold in every role, team, or environment:

_____

_____

_____

_____

✦ For each one, write the consequence of what happens when it's violated and how you respond:

Example:

Integrity

Consequence: Erodes trust with team

Response: Immediate accountability conversation + documented next steps

Worksheet 3: Accountability in Action

Use this framework to prepare for accountability conversations.

1. Describe the observed behavior or issue without judgment.

2. Reaffirm the standard and why it matters.

3. Ask for their perspective and listen.

4. Collaborate on a clear next step or improvement plan.

5. Document the follow-up plan and timeline.

Reflection

✦ What's the goal of this conversation?

_____

_____

_____

_____

✦ What mindset do you want to lead with: Clarity? Empathy? Resolve?

_____

_____

_____

_____

Worksheet 4:
Team Alignment Exercise

Ask your team these questions to realign and recommit to shared expectations:

- What are the top 3 standards that define our culture?

- What's something we've allowed that no longer aligns with who we are?

- Where do we need to tighten up or recommit?

- How do we hold each other accountable in a way that builds trust, not fear?

Write your personal commitment to the team here:

As your leader, I commit to:

_____

_____

_____

_____

SECTION 5:

Redefining Success

Make It Mean Something.

Worksheet 1:
My Definition of Success
(Right Now)

Success evolves. So should your definition.

✦ In your own words, describe what success looks like in this current season of your life:

_____

_____

_____

_____

✦ What would success feel like, not just look like, if you fully stepped into it this year?

_____

_____

_____

_____

Worksheet 2:
Then vs. Now

Reflect on how your view of success has changed over time.

✦ When I first started leading, I believed success meant:

_____

_____

_____

_____

✦ Now, I believe success means:

_____

_____

_____

_____

✦ What I let go of:

_____

_____

_____

_____

✦ What I now prioritize:

_____

_____

_____

_____

Worksheet 3:
Impact Over Numbers

Think about a moment in your career or business when you felt proud, not because of performance, but because of purpose.

✦ Describe that moment. What happened? Who was impacted? How did it make you feel?

_____

_____

_____

_____

✦ Why did that moment define success for you?

_____

_____

_____

_____

Worksheet 4:
30-Day Success Map

Let's make success personal and measurable on *your* terms.

Area of Focus	Goal / Outcome	Why It Matters	How You'll Measure It
Personal Growth			
Business or Career			
Team or Leadership			
Wellness or Peace			
Relationships or Legacy			

Worksheet 5: Who Am I Elevating?

One of the truest signs of leadership success is the elevation of others.

✦ List 3 people you've helped grow or guide in the last year. What changed for them because of you?

1. Name:

_____

Growth or Result:

_____

_____

2. Name:

_____

Growth or Result:

_____

_____

3. Name:

_____

Growth or Result:

_____

_____

✦ How did supporting their elevation align with
   your purpose?

_____

_____

_____

_____

SECTION 6:

4S Recap + Commitment

Apply It. Live It. Lead With It.

Worksheet 1:
My 4S Self-Assessment

Rate yourself in each area from 1 to 5 (1 = Needs Focus, 5 = Leading Strong). Be honest and use this as a checkpoint, not a judgment.

Pillar	Self-Rating (1–5)	Why You Chose This Rating	One Way You'll Grow in This Area
Support			
Strive			
Standards			
Success			

Worksheet 2:
Write Your 4S Manifesto

Use this space to write your own version of The 4S Manifesto, a statement of how you intend to lead, grow, and show up using this framework.

Start with:

I commit to leading with Support by...
I will continue to Strive by...
I will protect my Standards by...
I define Success as...

_____

_____

_____

_____

_____

Sign it like a contract with yourself.

Signature: _____

Date: _____

Worksheet 3:
Power Moves Plan

✦ What are 3 bold, intentional moves you will
make in the next 90 days that align with
The 4S Framework?

1. _____

_____

_____

2. _____

_____

_____

3. _____

_____

_____

✦ How will you keep yourself accountable?

- ☐ Keeping a personal journal

- ☐ Scheduling weekly calendar check-ins

- ☐ Partnering with an accountability buddy

- ☐ Booking a session or joining our leadership community

_____

_____

_____

Worksheet 4:
Stay Connected

You've done the inner work. Now continue the outer impact.

- **Visit** www.stacieselise.com

- **Book** a Power Session to go deeper

- **Subscribe** to The Stacie Selise Vault

- **Join the Community** to get access to upcoming events and leadership tools

- **Follow** @stacieselise on Instagram, LinkedIn, Facebook, and Threads

- **Share Your Journey:**
  Use the #The4SFramework hashtag or tag me directly. I'd love to hear your story

- **Scan the QR code below** to grab your copy of The 4S Framework by Stacie Selise playbook:

Your Leadership Journey Isn't Over, It's Just Beginning.

You now have the tools. You now have the language. You now have the framework.

Lead with it.

Build with it.

Live with it.

With power and purpose,

Stacie Selise

About the Author

Stacie Selise is a powerhouse in every sense of the word.

She is an award-winning former corporate executive turned entrepreneur, speaker, and executive leadership strategist. With over a decade of experience leading high-performing teams across the country, Stacie has mastered the art of people-centered leadership, culture transformation, and driving results without compromising integrity.

Born and raised in New York City, she built her career from the ground up, starting as a frontline employee and rising to become one of the top-performing leaders in a Fortune 20 company. Her journey from corporate leadership to launching her own consulting brand is rooted in real experience, resilience, and an unshakable belief in her purpose.

As the founder of The Stacie Selise Group and creator of The 4S Framework by Stacie Selise™, she equips leaders, entrepreneurs, and organizations with tools to lead with clarity, confidence, and vision.

Stacie's work is about more than motivation. It's about transformation. She is committed to building legacy through leadership and helping others define success on their own terms.

To connect, visit *www.stacieselise.com*
Follow *@stacieselise* on all platforms
Join the movement. Lead with purpose.

www.ingramcontent.com/pod-product-compliance
Lightning Source LLC
Chambersburg PA
CBHW070353130626
46556CB00007B/3155